I0486124

Business Continuity as a Career? Really?

Building a World Class BC Program and Career

Howard M. Peace

Howard M. Peace
206 Cedarview Dr
Asheville, NC 28803
www.peacebusinesscontinuity.com

Ordering Information:
Quantity sales. Special discounts are available on quantity purchases by corporations, associations, and others. For details, contact the "Special Sales Department" at the address above.

Business Continuity as a Career? Really?/ Howard M. Peace. —1st ed.
ISBN 978-1517290528

CONTENTS

INTRODUCTIONS

Before asking you to plunge into this tome, let me introduce myself and the story behind the book:

About the Author: I have been involved with disaster recovery and business continuity planning for over 30 years. (Yes, I started as a small child.) Along the years I have been blessed to help move the role of the BC/DR planner from someone who wasn't busy enough in the data center to the level of certified professionalism and corporate-wide scope it enjoys today. Originally, DR for me involved moving a cartload of tapes down the block in NYC from Manufacturers Hanover Trust (Manny Hanny) to Chemical Bank to run a few applications on their mainframe on the third shift. Eventually, we financed the building of Comdisco's Carlstadt, NJ facility and set up recovery there. The early planning packages were clumsy and used a TSO edit type of word processing that produced ugly, but workable documents. Then around 1985 I came across a man in Tampa who had a new package called LDRPS that actually allowed you to use any word processing and database package to produce great looking documents and a whole new software industry was born.

The idea of planning for business units was presented to me as I stood on the sidewalk with my boss in front of Manny Hanny's Park Avenue location during a fire drill in 1984. Jack Evans, the Deputy General Manager at MHT, approached us and said, "If we can't go back into the building, what are you going to do about all those specialized foreign currency exchange terminals on the third floor?" And our mission was expanded.

Over the years I've watched as the movement out of the glass house came with distributed computing, then back to the glass house as that dried up. Then the advent of PC's hit and we had mission critical applications being developed and housed all around the buildings, more often than not, sitting under the department secretary's desk without the benefit of security or generator support.

But eventually, information systems got their act together and the modern infrastructure we now enjoy emerged. Along the way, BC/DR matured as well and now is concerned with systems, applications, network, voice, facilities, and manufacturing processes across the corporation's footprint around the globe. It's been a great ride.

I stumbled into consulting because Ernst & Young wanted to buy some of my vacation time to help out a client of theirs. Several years later I launched Peace of Mind Consulting, struck out on my own, and managed to do some good work for clients like General Shale, Cracker Barrel, Unisys, and others. Eventually, Comdisco came along with an offer that didn't require me to move to Philadelphia and I worked for them until layoffs hit. I relaunched Peace of Mind Consulting and worked for clients like Crestar Bank, First Union National Bank, Cisco Systems, and various others. I even got to do some bank risk reviews for Lloyds of London in Latin America and Saudi Arabia.

In 2001 I took a job with VeriSign because they threw a bunch of stock options and a California apartment at me. That lasted 18 months as the stock price dropped from $52 to $5 and my options were so far underwater that Jacques Cousteau couldn't find them. Next I got a chance to build a business continuity consulting practice for Avaya that also included oversight of some of the brightest information security consultants anywhere. After 3 years of that, I was approached by CyberTrust to build a similar practice there as well as refine their security and compliance practice methodologies. Verizon bought us and I wound up there for the next 8 years developing all the business continuity consulting methodologies, training sales teams, and managing projects for Fortune 500 clients and government entities like FDNY, the city of Los Angeles, and the Marines.

And now, I'm back on my own, only the name "Peace of Mind Consulting" is now owned by someone else, so it's Peace Business Continuity. I've had a wonderful career so far, had a chance to work with and for some of the brightest of the bright, travel the world, and be involved with the birth and development of the field of BC/DR. Not too shabby, I think.

About the Book: The roots of this book can be found in the blogs I began to write for both LinkedIn and my website, **www.peacebusinesscontinuity.com**. After writing several blogs, my wife said, "You should write a book". Being the typical husband, I ignored her at first. But after a while, I had to admit that I really enjoyed writing about my experiences in the industry. I looked through all the books available on

Amazon and so many of them read like college text books, full of useful information, but a little dry and humorless. There were tons of charts, references to standards, and good project planning ideas, but lacking, perhaps, in soul. So I decided there was room for my ruminations in the marketplace.

In this book I have tried to share what I consider are important aspects of working successfully in the field. The observations run from the general to the very specific and always include real world examples of using the tools of the trade, like the Business Impact Analysis (BIA), a comprehensive recovery strategy for both the technical and business areas, positioning BC/DR for the best chance of mission success within the organization, hiring staff, using BC consultants effectively, and conducting successful table top exercises. My professional motto is "***Consulteo ergo sum – I consult, therefore I am***", so feel free to reach out to me via email, the phone, or visit my website. I hope you have as much fun reading this as I had in writing it. Happy reading.

CHAPTER 1

BUSINESS CONTINUITY AS A CAREER? REALLY?

Yes, really! For a lot of good reasons, some of which I'll discuss here. I admit I fell into it quite accidently. I was an honest programmer once, coding away in Assembly Language and COBOL in my youth. But the bank where I was working needed some information security programming done, then a security administrator for the Money Transfer and Wire department, and before I knew it I got moved uptown and became one of the first CISO's in the country. Along the way, they told me there was this thing called business continuity and disaster recovery and it was going to report to me, too, so I'd better get up to speed on that as well. In that way, I was fortunate to participate in the evolution of a discipline that grew from just getting the lights to blink at the recovery center to addressing recovery needs for the business units across the globe. It's been a great ride and here is why I think business continuity (BC) makes for a potentially great career.

You can see forever from here. The view from a cubicle in most departments is limited to only a small part of the overall business a corporation conducts. You'll get an in depth familiarity with that department's business, but that's all. Whereas, working in BC will expose you to everything the corporation does: all the business processes in every department, the assets, technology, locations, future plans, etc. It's a stepladder in the cubicle farm!

You meet the nicest people. Working in BC you will come in close contact with all the decision makers in the company. You'll have regular interaction with department managers, middle management, and senior managers from across the corporation, many of whom you would never even have a conversation with at a company picnic. In your exposure to them you'll learn their priorities, their vision, their management style, etc. You'll also get a seat at the table for crisis management as they enact the plans you have developed. You'll have a chance to shine in arenas you'd never be invited to otherwise, which can only help your career.

You get to do important work. Enlightened corporations and management recognize the essential part business continuity plays in ensuring the availability of technology, telecommunications, facilities, and staff resources in order to continue mission critical activities. The role you play in analyzing business and technical recovery requirements, creating workable plans for recovery from unexpected outages, and testing recovery capabilities can be the difference between full recovery and huge potential losses. That's pretty important stuff!

You can qualify for professional certification. Years ago I got a phone call from an important figure in the field offering me a chance to have my certification grandfathered in for a mere $1,000. I declined because I thought the certification wasn't worth the paper it was written on (and I didn't have a spare $1,000). But all that has changed over the years to the point where the certification process is both professional and valuable. The testing process and in-field work experience required now represent a mark of achievement and has gained recognition as the distinction of a highly qualified professional in an exacting discipline. I'm proud to have the CBCP after my name. (On a side note, I once had a translator in Mexico City who had PDG after his name on his business card. I asked him what that meant and he said, "Oh, I gave myself that and nobody ever asks what it means. It stands for Pretty Damned Good", but he wasn't and I fired him after two days.)

You get to put your thinking cap on. Solving the problems of providing sufficient recovery capabilities that meet the business requirements in the timeframes needed at the lowest possible cost is a daunting challenge. New technologies, changing business requirements, new recovery vehicles (like cloud computing), and changing priorities will always present new obstacles to overcome. Succeeding in managing these well will keep the juices flowing.

Conclusion. Even if your neighbors don't understand what the heck you do for a living, you'll know it's challenging, ever changing, and important.

Enjoy BC and have some fun out there!

CHAPTER 2

THE TOP 10 COMPONENTS OF A CORPORATE BUSINESS CONTINUITY PROGRAM

So you're a lousy ducker and your boss just decided to assign you another responsibility: building an internal Business Continuity Program for your company. Like you don't already have a fulltime job, maybe several. Lucky you, really. I say lucky because now you have a chance to build something from the ground up that will have significant impact in every area of the company. Do it right and you'll know more about what the company does with technology, operations, business functions, and risk management than almost anyone. As I always tell newbies, BCP is a great way to look for your next internal job because you'll see into every department, spot the up and coming areas, and figure out where you wouldn't want to work or work for! You'll also be ready to embark on a whole new career in an exciting field somewhere else, if you so choose.

Having built world class BCP programs at Cisco, First Union National Bank, and Verisign, and having built successful BC consulting practices at Peace Business Continuity, Avaya, and Verizon, I think I might be able to offer some useful suggestions. So don't panic, here are what I consider to be the 10 most important elements you'll need to include in your new adventure:

1. **Business Impact Analysis (BIA)**. The BIA is the most important tool you can use to determine the most critical business processes and the technology infrastructure on which they depend to continue essential activities during an unexpected outage. A properly conducted BIA will help you determine recovery priorities, based on the impacts experienced in the business units, so the recovery strategies you implement will ensure the most critical needs are addressed first. Think of the BIA as a step ladder in a cubicle farm. By conducting data gathering interviews with the decision makers in each silo, you'll be asking important questions about:

    a. <u>All business activities performed by the business unit</u> ("tell me about what you do here")

b. <u>The resources that are required to support these activities</u> ("tell me about what you need from infrastructure, applications, databases, phones, and physical locations")

c. <u>The impacts, over time, of an unexpected outage of these resources</u> ("what happens if you lose any, or all, of these resources for half a day, one day, two days, etc.)

d. <u>The interaction between other business areas</u> (tell me about where your input comes from and where your output goes)

By asking these type of questions a picture will emerge that details the possible effects an unexpected outage will have on the business units' ability to continue mission critical functions over various periods of time. An additional benefit for your BCP Program is that you will be doing what I like to call "Evangelizing among the heathen". You will raise awareness levels about the risks imposed by outages to their ability to function as expected. And when you come back later to talk about developing business continuity plans they will understand the importance of what you are doing and will be far more willing to cooperate.

2. **Recovery Gap Analysis**. The results of the BIA should provide you with what mission critical activities must be recovered first, and how soon. Now it's time to examine the capability of the current state infrastructure to recover these critical functions within the timeframes required, if at all. For example, let's say you determine the call center provides an essential service to the company and there is no backup plan in place. Or maybe there is somewhere to fail over calls but the secondary location cannot support the call volume effectively, or doesn't have access to essential data bases and support software needed to make answering the phones effective.   Ouch!   You've uncovered a gap that must be remediated. Or let's say you uncover an application that supports mission critical functions that has no recovery server available to run the app at an offsite location. Again, ouch! The value of the data gathered in your analysis is that

you are now able to spot technical roadblocks, or shortfalls in effective recovery support. The output from the Gap Analysis will provide the input necessary to design a future state infrastructure recovery capability.

3. **Technology Topography**. I can't tell you how many clients I have asked for a topography from who look like deer in the headlights. "We have a network diagram and a server list. Is that good enough?" No, because no one has ever put on paper what is being run on every server and what business areas they support. The data from the BIA will allow your technology group to map exactly how that technology supports mission critical business activities, maybe for the first time ever. The input to their disaster recovery planning is invaluable for creating a recovery strategy that is more effective and may suggest a need for infrastructure upgrades, like a move to virtualized servers and possible cloud recovery options.

4. **Recovery Strategy Definition**. With the BIA and Gap Analysis data in hand, you can now work with both the technology and business groups to come up with meaningful recovery strategies that will allow recovery within the needed timeframes. You may not be able to meet all those requirements with the current state infrastructure, but you will have the necessary information to make reasonable risk management decisions about how best to proceed.

5. **Backup and Change Management Strategies**. You'll need to closely examine both of these to make sure critical data is available at the offsite location, (especially for those functions requiring immediate failover capabilities) and that any system or application changes in the primary data center are reflected in the secondary location in a timely fashion, with complete and accurate documentation. (Remember you're dealing with the sons and grandsons of mainframe system programmers- "We don't need no stinking documentation.")

6. **Planning Tools**. At some point you're going to have to decide the method that will be used to write disaster recovery and business continuity plans. There are some really good tools out there that you can research and some really complicated ones that require training and vendor support. Here are some points to consider:

   a. Vendor supplied tools can be complicated and may require you to send someone for offsite training. The downside is they will have to run the software, do most or all of the input, and may leave you hanging by going somewhere else and you're suddenly back to square one.

   b. Much of the data you will need to include in the plans is already being maintained by someone else somewhere else, like production libraries. They will not take kindly to having to rekey everything in to your little tool and will tend to "forget" to keep it current. Instead use a tool that can be pointed to those libraries at time of execution.

c. Everybody knows how to use Word and Excel, so why not use them. Think about designing templates, or buy them online, and using them to capture your data and procedures.

7. **Written Disaster Recovery and Business Continuity Plans**. I can't tell you how many clients I have run into that do not have fully documented plans in place. "Everybody knows what needs to be done so why bother to write it down?" This, of course, is a bad idea on many levels. First, everybody doesn't know what needs to be done, maybe not even their own small part. Secondly, everybody may not be available for the recovery, including key staff who are the holders of the tribal knowledge (think of vacations, injuries, regional disasters, etc.). And finally, because nobody knows everything and how it all fits together, coordination of critical activities across departmental silos may be ineffective or impossible. On a side note, don't allow yourself to get roped into writing all the plans for all the areas. You already have a full plate and if you do this, you will be ground down to a

nub.   Provide   the   tools,   training, consulting,   and   tracking   so   the responsibility resides where it belongs. They will tend to take ownership of their plan much more readily than if you write their plan for them, especially in the business areas.

8. **Tabletop Exercises**. Make frequent use of tabletop exercises to walk through the plans   with   those   responsible   for execution at time of disaster. This is the subject of another chapter in this book, but let me give you the highlights that make these exercises an indispensable part of your BC Program:

    a. Plan the scope of the test carefully (don't boil the ocean, limit your target)

    b. Determine what a successful test looks like (finding holes is a good thing)

    c. Educate the participants on what to expect (or they won't show up)

    d. Create   a   meaningful   outage scenario that could really happen (So, Mars attacks...)

    e. Keep the scenario secret (real disasters,   except   maybe

hurricanes, don't come with warnings)
f. Keep the exercise on track (someone always wants to take over)
g. Walkthrough the plans as written
h. Record any open issues or missing documentation
i. End on time
j. Write an after action report that describes the exercise and results (include all open issues and who is responsible for resolution and when)
k. Update the plan (there will be issues, I promise)

9. **Recovery Testing Program**. I always tell my clients, "Every watch is waterproof until you dunk it." The very first time you exercise your recovery plan should never be during an actual disaster. That's a prescription for failure and no matter what goes wrong, you know whose face will have egg on it. Successful tests take a great deal of careful prior planning involving both technology and business functions. Set a

reasonable scope with clear objectives, involve the appropriate parties, set realistic time objectives, and document everything so you can update the plan. As always, write an after action report. My advice is to always start with limited failover tests to build on for the future. Testing can be scary, but you'll never know if you can do it until you do it. (More on testing in future blogs on the website.)

10. Awareness Program. The greatest BC Program in the world will fail if nobody in house knows about it, or you. Set up an intranet page with all kinds of pertinent information on the Program, access to the tools and templates, testing schedule, status, future plans, and general BC/DR information. A blurb from senior management about their support is helpful also. Your goal is to educate the company on the important work you are doing and what is expected of them.

Okay, long chapter I know, but I hope it has been helpful. Please feel free to submit comments or contact me. I've been where you are and I lived to tell the tale, so good luck and much success! You can do this!

CHAPTER 3

WHERE SHOULD BCP REPORT AND TO WHOM?

As a consultant, I get asked this question a lot. Either when a client is in the process of establishing a new function, or they have become disenchanted with the results they are getting, or they are having problems getting cooperation or visibility for the Program. Usually, however, they ask the question wrong. They ask where it should report, or who it should report to, but miss the fact that it is really a two part question. As with any business function, where BCP reports can be as problematic as having the wrong management overseeing it, so it's both where and to whom. Allow me to discuss some of the pros and cons and offer some general guidance on the proper placement of the BCP function which will help ensure its best opportunity for success.

Where should BCP report? I've encountered successful BCP functions reporting at numerous places in the organization. Frequently, it resides in the technology department, but quite often it sits under other more general business functions, such as administration, treasury, project management, physical security, or facilities.   Wherever it sits, it must have the following to be successful:

- **It should report somewhere where it won't get lost**.   In highly complex organizations where there a multitude of foci, it is more difficult to bubble up the important BCP issues to the top for proper attention to detail.   So much noise is generated with everyone else's issues that the voice of one crying in the wilderness receives little or no attention. Meeting agendas are so clogged that BCP issues are saved for last and often get short shrift, or they run out of time before they can be even addressed.
- **It should not report too high in any organization**. I've seen it report to the CIO, the CFO, or the COO and watched as those busy managers just had too much on their plates to give BCP any but the slightest attention. Better to have a reasonable chain of command that can get on their calendar when necessary with an agenda properly focused on what BCP needs.
- **It should not report too low in any organization**. If BCP sits too far down

the chain the relevant issues won't ever bubble up and the decision process will become overly onerous and long. Sitting too low says to the rest of the organization that BCP isn't very important and the BC manager doesn't rate as someone they should listen to. What you're looking for is "just right", like in the story of the three bears. Close enough to decision makers to get the right amount of attention but not so low that BCP gets drowned out by everything else. And "just right" is different in every organization. Like Goldilocks, you'll figure it out.

- **It should not report to the audit department**. Audit's role is to ensure an organization's processes and documentation comply with internal and external policies and requirements. In effect, they check the work of others. Implementing the BC Program themselves removes their ability to objectively review the content and procedures of the BCP. While they might have some great ideas and tribal knowledge to offer, they should refrain from direct responsibility for implementation, freeing them to fulfill their charter. Any smart BC Manager will maintain open communication and cooperation with audit, but it is my opinion that the reporting of BCP should be placed elsewhere in the organization.

- **The reporting structure should include BCP accountability**. Most organizations use a management by objective (MBO) accountability for managers that will be used to measure personal success for the year. Having a personal MBO for the success of the BCP function reporting to them does wonders to focus attention and provides incentive to ensure BCP gets the cooperation it needs both inside their realm and across the company.

- **Reporting to Technology is sometimes problematic**. Sometimes locating BCP in Technology sends the message to the rest of the organization that BCP is primarily, maybe completely, a technology problem, in effect just disaster recovery. Get the systems up and running and everything will be fine. Not. Years ago, getting the lights blinking at the recovery center in Philadelphia was all we in disaster recovery had to worry about. In the years since, especially after 9/11, the mission has expanded to include everything else. A correctly implemented BCP must address outage issues residing in the business functions, facilities, remote locations, assembly lines, and on and on. Locating the BCP in Technology sometimes clouds organization thinking about extending disaster recovery beyond the data center to include true business continuity.

• **Not reporting to Technology is sometimes problematic**. Contrarily, reporting to a non-technology area can lead to barriers in communicating with the technical staff and management. (I've had sys admins and DBA's talk slow to me like English was my second language until I explained I was one of them once, before I went over to the dark side.) BCP can be viewed as an outside organization that really couldn't understand the massive undertaking of recovery and is there to lay more burdens on an already over worked and underfunded technology group. If it reports elsewhere, the BCP group must work hard to build relationships and earn respect to gain cooperation. They should acknowledge what they don't know, ask good questions and listen to the answers, and show appreciation when they ask already busy people to do one more damned thing, for them.

To whom should BCP report? Now we're getting to the other side of the equation. In all honesty, I'd rather have BCP report to the right person in almost any area in the company than the "right" organization with the "wrong" person in charge. Why? Because the right manager can accomplish BCP initiatives wherever he or she sits in the organization. He knows how to get things done, has a solid reputation, knows and is known by the right people, and knows how to manage for success. Here are some things to consider when choosing who should manage BCP reporting (I'll be using "he" instead of he/she for convenience, but I have seen and worked for great managers of both sexes):

- **He should understand the importance of BCP**. Having had the additional function plopped on his plate, he should endeavor to educate himself in the BCP mission and issues. He must learn to recognize the critical importance of BCP and be prepared to devote as much time and effort as necessary to accomplish success for his new reports.

The "wrong" manager will think little of the importance of his new function and won't even learn how to spell BCP, much less acquire the knowledge to speak intelligently to senior management about it.

- **He should be well versed in the corporate tribal knowledge.** Knowing the inner workings of the organization as a whole will enable him to guide the BCP staff in accomplishing their mission. He will know how things are supposed to work, how they really work, and understands the difference. Each company is unique and speaks their own language (I once was corrected at MBNA that they referred to employees as their "people", not "staff"). He will also know who the right decision makers are, how to approach them, how and when to report status to them, etc.

- **He must be able to open the right doors for BCP.** A successful BCP requires access to highly placed decision makers and the new reporting manager must be able to open doors to the executive suite at appropriate times and with actionable information they need to see. He should command their respect and use that influence to garner a spot on their calendar. He will also know what BCP needs to attain visibility, such as which meetings to be invited to, which email lists to be included on, what memos to read, and how to acquire a place on other managers' agendas. He should be able to smooth the way for his new staff to interact with senior leaders of other areas that are important to the success of their mission. Sort of virtue by association.

- **He should be a good manager and coach.** He will have to evaluate the strengths and weaknesses of his new staff and determine how best to deploy them. In some, he will recognize their ability to interface successfully with senior management. Others he will determine are better suited to background roles. He should also evaluate their technology knowledge, writing ability, and company business awareness and make plans to fill in the blanks, perhaps using his education budget. As a coach, he should be an encourager to keep spirits up in the face of the adversity they will face and keep the focus sharp on the objectives that will make BCP successful.

Placing a BCP function in the right reporting structure and under the right manager is worth the time and effort and will go a long way toward enabling their success. Both where, and to whom, should be equally considered, and every company is different. I wish you success as you make your determination and welcome any comments on this chapter at my website.

CHAPTER 4

USING THE BIA TO BUILD THE BUSINESS CASE FOR BC/DR

I admit it, I'm a BIA bigot. I've been doing them since 1980 and I've never found a more effective tool in building the business case that convinces senior management that BC/DR is important, worth the investment, and essential to corporate survival. A properly conducted BIA will provide the following business case data:

- A more thorough understanding of the business and all of its components. **Think of it as stepladder in the cubicle farm**. Most organizations are fairly complex and consist of silos of business and technical activity. The BIA should include interviews with each component and will provide an overview of essential activities that will need to continue in the face of an unexpected outage. It will also gather in one place, sometimes for the first time ever, the identification of the complete technical resources required to support ongoing business processes, the interrelationships between business functions, and an understanding of the progressive degradation of critical functionality over time.

- <u>The impacts of outages on critical business functions</u>. The BIA should be used to measure how well a business area can continue operating with the loss of some or all of its critical resources. The impacts should be estimated using parameters on operations, revenue, costs, obligations, customer impact, and corporate reputation. The effects should be measured over time so the impacts can be graphed and presented to management.

- <u>The identification of critical business processes</u>. Every department has a mix of critical and non-essential or deferrable functions. The BIA interviews should be used to separate out those activities which support the most critical activities from those that a delay would have little or no impact. Once the most critical activities have bubbled to the surface, a recovery strategy to address those in a timely fashion can be developed. These critical activities are usually the ones which have the highest level of impact, whether it be financial, operations, or negative customer effects.

- Recovery time objectives (RTO). A general rule of thumb is the more immediate the recovery, the more it costs and the more complicated recovery becomes. The BIA should identify the timeframes in which the outage increases the impact on critical functions to an unacceptable level. In the BIA methodology I have developed over the years I use an impact scale that rises from a score of zero (no impact at all) to a five (OMG, hair on fire, this is really, really bad). A good interviewer tries to talk the business representative off the ledge (Is it really a 5 at a half day of outage, or maybe only a 3?), but there will be activities that rise to the highest level of impact in a very short time. This information allows me to draw a pie chart that shows which functions require, in effect, immediate failover recovery and those that need to be recovered in the 24, 48, 72, and 96 plus hours timeframe. The chart becomes a great tool to use in the development of recovery strategies to meet the timeframe requirements, perhaps using different options for each slice.

- Identification of gaps in the current state recovery capabilities. By now we know how fast the various critical functions need to recovered to reduce the effect of an outage. It's time now to examine the infrastructure's ability to meet those demands. For example, let's say you discover a critical function must be recovered at an offsite location in 4 hours or less, but there is no server available there to support such a quick recovery. Or you uncover the fact that the database needed to support the application will take 96 hours to recover from tape, blowing your RTO out of the water if the most current data is not already there. Or you discover that failing over critical calls to another call center would extend wait times to an unacceptable level, thereby violating contract agreements. The good news is the BIA has identified gaps in the recovery capability that can be addressed. The Gap Analysis section of the BIA should include the costs and implementation efforts for the remedy and will provide the business case for doing so in a timely fashion.

- <u>Input for the development of future state recovery</u>. This is the part where a good BIA marries the critical business activities and outage information, the RTO's, and the Gap Analysis to create a high level roadmap of where the organization should be heading if they want to increase their recovery capabilities to an acceptable level. The data from the BIA can be used to influence both infrastructure and business planning. For example, the shortfalls in the Gap Analysis might be addressed by an upgrade in the offsite capabilities, a change in the timing and content of backups of critical data, or a move to virtual servers. It's possible an organization could now justify splitting the data center between two locations with the capability of mutual recovery for critical resources. Or they could decide to use the pie chart to plan to provide for immediate failover needs in a co-location space while using a cloud arrangement for the more deferrable recovery requirements, thereby saving cost without increasing risks. Likewise, the BIA data can influence business planning to support decisions to outsource certain functions, split physical locations to reduce risk, or to simplify certain business processes.

With all the data collected, analyzed, and digested, a business case can be developed that outlines the threat, presents the business impacts over time, details the timeframes for recovery of critical functionality, identifies the gaps in recovery capabilities, and provides the makings of a high level roadmap that includes the effort and expense of increasing recovery capabilities to an acceptable risk posture. If you've done an effective BIA, the way forward should be much clearer and you've been able to build a persuasive business case that gives senior management the data it needs to make a good technical, business, and financial decisions.

I have used the BIA over and over again as the critical first step in determining what has to be recovered and how fast it must be accomplished. It is the perfect tool to educate management on the importance of disaster recovery and business continuity planning. Seeing the results should convince them that with all the other squeaky wheels asking for oil out there, this is one for which they need to provide funds and support.   Enjoy doing a BIA!

CHAPTER 5

THE USE OF THE **BIA** TO ESTABLISH TIER REQUIREMENTS FOR RECOVERY STRATEGIES

The Business Impact Analysis (BIA) methodology espoused in an earlier chapter provides the information for correctly determining recovery priorities for the underlying applications and infrastructure. A further useful addition would be to then divide the results into Tiers, each with its own specific requirements. For example, a high rating in impact would indicate that a rapid recovery capability must be in place, perhaps calling for a designation as **High Availability**. Such quick recovery would require the equipment and communications links to already be in place in the remote recovery facility and the data would have to be as near to current as possible, perhaps through replication and mirroring. Associating those requirements by Tiers for new and existing services has the benefit of ensuring:

- The equipment and communications links are in place

- Appropriate replication methods were available
- Sufficient budget was allocated (especially for new services)
- The growth in adequate technical resources could be properly managed

The Tier terminology can be determined in whatever nomenclature makes sense to the company. (You may want to dig out the designations that were used for Y2K for a start.) But for an example we will use the following:

- Tier A: failover must occur in under 4 hours (High Availability)
- Tier B: recovery must occur in under 24 hours
- Tier C: recovery must occur within 3 days
- Tier D: recovery must occur within 7 days
- Tier E: recovery should occur within 14 days

Obviously, each of these tiers require different provisions, some ahead of time, others at a more leisurely pace after the higher tiers have been restored, and only when an extended outage is expected.

The BIA could be used to determine tiers by the results of the scoring of the impact outages have on the business unit's ability to continue mission critical functions.   Let's look at an example:

New service X is proposed. The business case is developed for it by the business unit, Information Technology is requested to design a solution, and the BIA is conducted. The results indicate a high impact effect of extended outages, earning it a Tier A designation. Having done so, the following requirements are obvious if it can be recovered in time to avoid the unacceptable impacts:

- Local failover
- Remote failover
- Data replication
- DR plan for the application and databases
- BC plan for the business unit
- Table top tests for the BC and DR
- Limited Failover testing

All of these requirements fall out of the designation as a Tier A. Therefore, adequate technical planning can occur and the budget process will have to make provision for **both** the production and recovery configurations before approval.

The table below is an example and will have to be adjusted for the company's needs:

Service	BIA Score	Tier	RTO	Recovery Requirements
X	95	A	< 4 hours	Local failover, remote failover, data replication, DR plan, BC plan, tabletop tests, limited failover test
Y	88	B	< 24 hours	Same as above
Z	79	C	< 3 days	Remote failover, tape backup,, DR plan, BC plan, Tabletop tests
N	65	D	< 7 days	Tape backup, DR & BC plans and tabletops
M	55	E	< 14 days	Same as above

With these requirements known during the planning process, all the benefits listed above accrue and all the costs are known. The reasoning for doing this is as follows:

- **The total cost of the project is known.** If the application is rated Tier

A, equipment and licenses are obtained for both the primary and the fall back configurations. Going back to the well for money later for the backup configuration may result in a lack of funding for recovery.

- **The total scope of the project is known**. A project plan that includes both installations and testing is developed to reflect the real scope of effort required.

- **Impacts on the infrastructure are known**. The effects of adding new primary and recovery configurations can be determined to make sure the network, backup methodology, and staff considerations are measured ahead of time. Upgrades and adjustments can be performed proactively rather in catch up mode later, if at all.

- **Revisions to the overall recovery strategy are known**. The changes will add new tasks to be performed which may adversely affect the recovery timeline. The new recovery requirements must be folded into the strategy seamlessly in order to preserve and even improve the company's recovery capability for all mission critical functions.

You may have noticed the use of scoring in the BIA results in the chart above, something we haven't talked about yet. I added scoring to my methodology when I was consulting at Cisco Systems in 2001. What I needed was a way to ensure that business functions that had a disparity in their impact measurements would properly show their relative overall impact. For example, let's take a customer-facing web application that is used to track build times and predict delivery schedules. The BIA outage ratings are as follows (on a 0 – 5 scale for a 2 day outage):

Outage Category	Outage Impact
Financial loss	0
Additional costs	0
Operations	2
Customer	5
Legal Obligations	0
Score	**7**

At first glance, this doesn't appear to be a very important application, probably a Tier D or E, meaning it would not be recovered in the first week. However, notice that the Customer Facing Impact is a 5, what I refer to as "OMG, hair on fire!" This impact rating was chosen by the business unit because they know

46

customers are heavy users of this web application to check on their orders, plan for implementation, schedule downtime, and staffing requirements for when it rolls in the door. Failure to provide this little app would have a detrimental impact on customer relations and could, in certain situations, cause the order to be cancelled, or at least effect future orders. Consider this scenario: An important customer has to call sales because the application is down and wants to know the status of his order, and all the salesman can tell him is, "The system is down, but I can let you know next Thursday, I think." Okay, so how do we handle this?

You have to understand that at Cisco I was dealing with hundreds of BIA's for thousands of applications and couldn't possible examine every result for anomalies like we just discovered with this web frontend. So, I decided to add a scoring element that could recognize anomalies like this. Yes, I know, all the statisticians out there are groaning about skewing the purity of the numbers, but it worked. See below:

Outage Category	Outage Impact	Outage Points	Weighted Score

Financial loss	0	10	0
Additional costs	0	10	0
Operations	2	10	20
Customer	5	15	75
Legal Obligations	0	10	0
Score	**7**		**95**

The weighted score is now 95, making it a Tier A application because of the direct customer impact it would have. Without increasing the Customer outage points to 15, it would have scored only as a 70, slotting it for recovery with the other Tier D's in a week, much to the detriment of customer relations.

Your environment might be much more simple than Cisco's was, but I thought this might be a valuable trick to add to your analysis if your situation is complicated enough to use it.

Summary. As you know, all applications are not equal. The BIA is designed to measure the relative impact outages have on mission critical business functions.   The analysis will show some as requiring highly available solutions, while others are more deferrable. The use of Tiers to designate the relative impact can then be used to pre-determine what recovery capabilities should be in place to support recovery within the critical timeframes. This is not only useful in developing workable recovery strategies but also in making sure new changes have been properly evaluated, slotted in the right Tiers, and the correct provisions for recovery have been budgeted and planned.

CHAPTER 6

DEVELOPING A BC/DR RECOVERY STRATEGY

This chapter involves the development of recovery strategies for both disaster recovery and business continuity. The needs of both the technical and business sides of the house must be addressed in a unifying strategy that provides a realistic capability of meeting the needs of the mission critical functions, within the timeframes required, using a realistic technological approach that is both effective and affordable. Wow, a mouthful, right? And that's the challenge.

Prior to attempting this I recommend that a comprehensive BIA be performed for determining priorities, outage impacts, and recovery requirements. The next step is to perform a Gap Analysis to determine what capability the current state technology environment has in meeting those requirements. Establishing s recovery strategy without this vital information is like setting out in a forest without a map and no clear idea of where you're going. You'll feel like you're making a certain amount of progress, but you won't have any idea if you'll arrive where you need to be until you emerge from the trees.

A properly conducted BIA should provide you with the following:

- A complete list of all the applications, servers, and underlying technology (like network connectivity, traffic, workspace, etc.) that each of the business functions require
- A good feel for how quickly those requirements need to be restored (Recovery Time Objectives -RTO's) based on the organization's ability to endure the pain from the outage
- An understanding of how much data can be lost, or how fast it can be recovered (Recovery Point Objectives – RPO's)
- An understanding of the priorities for restoration based on the relative impact the outages will have on mission critical functions (the big picture across the silos)
- An understanding of the interrelated dependencies (input, output) each business function has with the others
- The identification of deferrable items that can be addressed later in the recovery process

A properly conducted Gap Analysis will use the BIA information to examine the current state technology infrastructure and processes to determine the following:

- Do offsite recovery capabilities exist for supporting the recovery of all the applications, servers, and underlying technology?
- Can recovery be accomplished within the timeframes required?
- Is the data replication process sufficient to meet the RPO requirements?
- Is it possible to structure the recovery process to meet the business function priorities?
- Is there a way to take advantage of the deferrable items that will save time on the frontend?
- Are sufficient knowledgeable staff resources available to manage the recovery process (availability of key staff)?

As you can see, it gets complicated and requires a bird's eye view. There are companies that require almost immediate failover of all mission critical functions, such as airlines, banks, car rental agencies, etc. But in most business situations, some compromise must be reached. We'll look at the technical side of recovery first.

With the information you have gathered you should be able to draw a pie chart like the one below to illustrate the recovery timeframe requirements:

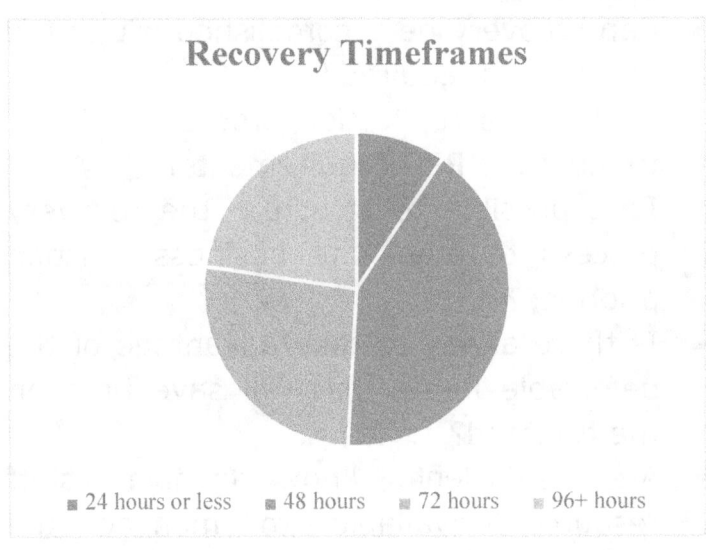

Recovery Timeframes

■ 24 hours or less   ■ 48 hours   ■ 72 hours   ■ 96+ hours

Your chart will be different, depending on the BIA results, but you will now be able to slot recovery into the pie slices and have a graphical representation of how much needs to be recovered how soon. For example, in the first hours of recovery no one focuses on the 96+ hour activities but they are heads down working on the High Availability and 48 hour items. Depending on how long the outage is expected to last, recovery of the more deferrable items might not even have begun before it is time to go home. The recovery strategy for technology should reflect these priorities and the business area recovery strategy should be constructed to reflect this timetable also.

Technology Recovery (often referred to as Disaster Recovery, as opposed to Business Continuity.)

You now have some options to examine for how best to recover the technology in the above timeframes:

For recovery in 24 hours or less: I refer to these functions as **High Availability**. These are functions for which an unexpected outage has serious consequences (such as financial losses, performance obligations, significant customer impact, etc.) Recovery must be fast, requires the most prior planning and staging of equipment, and it will not be cheap. The applications, servers, databases, and connectivity must be in place, and tested, and ready for failover as quickly as possible to mitigate the outage impacts. Obviously, there are a limited number of options available for meeting these time sensitive requirements. They include:

- A subscription-based service. This is provided by a number of vendors, including IBM and SunGard. A monthly fee is paid for a prescribed configuration of equipment and can include services like telecommunications hookups and data vaulting. Your subscription includes a set number of hours for testing annually. The drawbacks include the substantial monthly cost, scheduling sufficient testing time, travel costs, and the possibility that your configuration might be occupied when you need it due to disaster declarations by other customers. (The vendors usually have multiple sets of configurations and will do their best to accommodate you, but it might be in another physical location and can blow your recovery time schedule.) The advantage, of course, of a subscription-based service is that you don't have to buy the equipment, just rent it, whether you ever use it or not.
- Co-location space. This service is provided by a far larger number of conditioned-space vendors including Equinix, RackSpace, Corus360, and

others. They rent you the floor space, HVAC, telecommunications hookups, etc., and you provide the equipment. The monthly costs are lower, but savings are offset by the equipment capital outlay. The advantage is the guaranteed availability of the configuration to recover your highest requirements and the continued use of it to perform applications testing, system upgrades, load balancing with deferrable applications, etc. Some vendors, such as Verizon Terremark, will even bring up your systems for you negating the need for immediate travel.

- <u>Corporate-owned facility</u>. Many companies are opting to buildout their own space in facilities they already own. Considerations are the obvious cost, location on other power grids, availability of other telecommunications paths, shared weather-related threats, etc. All things considered, the ownership of the solution might be the right choice for your recovery strategy.

For recovery in 48 hours or less: The options for "second day" recovery aren't really a lot different for these "second tier" applications. You'll still have to stage equipment and data since the timely acquiring of emergency replacements for your primary configuration on such short notice is iffy, at best.   And don't forget how long it takes to restore data from backups because I have seen applications ready go in 48 hours but the database takes 96 hours to restore from tape. That's not something you want to explain to management at time of disaster!

For recovery in 72 hours. Now the options begin to open up for you.   If the business function can manage a three day outage, you might be able to acquire replacement equipment (planned for ahead of time, of course), configure the systems, load the applications and data, and spin them up in time.   If there are doubts about that happening, better to treat them like the higher priority items and stage recovery equipment and data for them.   Another option is the use of cloud configurations for virtual servers. Your vendor can spin those up for you and have them ready to bring online when needed.

For recovery in 96+ hours. Here is where, in my opinion, cloud computing presents the greatest opportunity for cost savings. I used to drive the cloud salesmen at Verizon crazy when I worked there, but "cloud" is a solution.

What's the problem it's supposed to fix? For deferrable applications, cloud computing is a perfect solution. It doesn't cost you anything until you use it and it can be ready in a flash, supposing the data is available. It's computing by the drink. And, of course, you now have the workable lead times to acquire replacement equipment on the fly for the deferrable slice of your pie.

Business Area Recovery Strategy. (often referred to as Business Continuity.)

Okay, we've looked at the strategic options for recovering the technology, but what are the business functions doing in the meantime? And what if the disaster dislocates them? We'll look at developing recovery strategies for business functions in two scenarios: recovery in place and relocation.

Recovery in Place for Business Functions. It's very possible that the unexpected outage will only effect the areas that house the technology component of the business, such as a fire in a data center or network nodes, etc. For most business areas, other than perhaps a brief period of facility evacuation, they can recover without having to physically move. During the BIA, each business area should have prioritized their workloads, looked at manual procedures, and considered how fast they needed to recovery mission critical functions. The outage impact discussions should have prepared them to develop a recovery strategy for their area to manage the delays caused by the unexpected outage and prepared them to recover operations as soon as the technology is restored. They may want to include in their strategy plans to add additional staff, shift workloads, notify interested parties, and confirm that systems have been properly restored.

Relocation of Business Functions. Now the business area recovery strategy gets much more complicated. If the business units need to abandon their normal locations, a careful mapping of where and when they are to arrive at their alternate work areas needs to be addressed from a global perspective. Without careful direction, multiple areas will plan on relocating to the cafeteria in the next building, take over the same conference rooms, and work from home without preparing for the additional network and system access requirements. In developing a Master Plan for relocation, the following items should be considered:

- **A Global Space Plan.** Mapping the recovery space from a global perspective is the only way to make sure everyone can be accommodated. Various iterations can be developed based on business cycles, partial relocation, extra staff, shift adjustments, etc. Any available work spaces will probably be scarce resources so it must be properly managed to meet the needs.
- **Priorities dictated by the Pie Chart.** In allocating space, the established recovery priorities must be taken into account in order to support the recovery timeframes. This should go a long way toward settling any territorial disputes. ("We got here first!")
- **Examine power and telecom requirements.** Make sure the backup space can handle the power and connectivity loads of the squatters. Putting people in a big open area, like a cafeteria, doesn't necessarily mean they can all plug their laptops in and get on the network. Also, you want to make sure the space is supported by the UPS and emergency generators, or your recovery activities could come to a screeching and uncomfortable halt.

- **Examine floor load capability.** If you're packing more weight per square foot than is normally expected you may run into structural support problems. A competent building engineer should be able to allay your fears or warn you off.
- **Plan for creature comforts.** You may have to make arrangements to feed staff, provide bottled water, set aside sleep areas, and provide for additional bathroom facilities.
- **Examine work styles.** One of the questions that should have been asked during the BIA was. "How collaborative is your department's work style?" What you're looking for is whether or not you can split the group between one or more recovery areas or do all have to be sitting together.
- **Work from home issues.** A certain number of business functions are already set up to work from home, alleviating the requirement to find corporate space for them. Others will think that is a great idea, but haven't arranged equipment and remote access for their staff. Again, it's a great question to ask during the BIA or at least when developing the business area recovery strategy. With

working from home, here are some
additional considerations:
- o Do they have reliable Internet
  access? For example, does it slow
  to a crawl when the neighborhood
  kids get off the school bus?
- o In a weather-related outage, do
  they have the power and Internet
  access they need?
- o Do they handle personal
  identifiable information (PII) where
  security might be compromised
  and are subject to federal
  standards? This information might
  include health records, credit
  cards, sensitive customer
  information, etc. If they process
  these kinds of transactions, work
  from home is not an option.
- o Do they have appropriate levels of
  antivirus software?
- **Voice support.** I always ask
  departments in my BIA work to tell me
  how they use dial tone. Provision has to
  be made for telephone access for the
  heavy users and call routing is a very
  important planning consideration.
- **Security issues.** Be aware of business
  functions handling PII or sensitive
  information that could be exposed to

prying eyes if they are not segregated appropriately. Also, you'll want to beef up your physical security presence to provide for escort to and from the parking lots as the staff works unusual hours.

- **Update floor evacuation plans.** The relocated staff need to be educated on escape plans, assembly areas, and new floor wardens need to be appointed and trained.

- **Use of vendor-supplied space.** Several vendors sell access to work area recovery centers. This is billed monthly on a per seat basis and can be configured to meet your needs.

- **Replacement equipment.** If you need to run out and get several hundred replacement PC's, you'd better have a plan in place to get them as quickly as possible. Also, since Dell doesn't ship PC's configured exactly as you want with your software pre-loaded, you need to figure in the manpower and time to set everything up to meet your time requirements.

Conclusion.   Long chapter, I know, but developing a workable recovery strategy that takes into account the recovery requirements for both the technology and business functions is a time consuming, but essential activity. You will have to involve information systems, network, voice, facilities, security, and senior management. As the old saying goes, "You need to know what needs to be done before you know whether or not you can do it." Laying out a unified strategy will go a long way toward making the tactical steps possible. Happy strategizing.

CHAPTER 7

DECISION MAKING AT TIME OF DISASTER

Every organization has their own structure and process for making decisions, especially those concerning the spending of money. However, when faced with an unexpected outage or disaster, things can change, sometimes unpredictably. Normal management processes can be completely disrupted depending on the nature of the event and the availability of the normal decision makers. For example, on 9-11, I had the exalted title of Director, Disaster Recovery and Business Continuance for a major technology company. Soon after the event began to unfold I found out that the CEO and CFO were on vacation together with their families and no one knew where. With air travel stopped dead and cell coverage overloaded, they were completely out of touch and unable to direct efforts to respond to the crisis. Additionally, almost all of the other senior management team were visiting a potential acquisition in another state and they were off the table also. In effect, the Facilities Manager and I were the only senior managers available to lead the crisis management efforts, and we were huddled around a small black and white TV trying to find out what was going on in the world. We soldiered on and made financial and management decisions normally above our pay grades and received confirmation that they were the correct decisions several days later when management came back on line. Afterward, I thought of a couple of items that should be included in our planning efforts. They are:

Management Succession Plans. In order to provide for the unavailability of key decision makers in a crisis, either personal or corporate, every manager should have a written management succession plan. Key leaders should formally identify who exactly should take over for them in their absence and what special authorities should be granted to them. (Remember Al Haig declared he was in charge when President Reagan was shot until someone reminded him that's not what the Constitution says.)   I developed my methodology when I was called in to consult with a family-owned Southern California Bank to write a plan for their IT Director. The Board had only recently found out his hobby was flying small acrobatic planes and they were worried that, God forbid, he crashed, no one knew what exactly he was working on or how to manage his department in his absence. After assuring him the Board wasn't looking to replace him, I was able to work with him to develop his first written job description, identify key staff who could assume most of his time-critical responsibilities, develop a written status report format and schedule, and improve his future planning documentation. I also interviewed him about his decision making methods and war gamed some scenarios to expose how he would likely respond if he were on duty. Lastly, I arranged for another senior manager to spend two days per month sitting with him getting up to speed on current state developments. In the end, the Board felt they had closed a major gap in their recovery planning efforts and used the methodology to create plans for other key roles as well.

Refined Tabletop Exercises. I am a firm believer in the usefulness of tabletop exercises in testing all facets of disaster recovery and business continuity plans. The exercise is a conference room based walkthrough of how a company will respond to an unexpected outage scenario revealed at the start of the exercise. The one wrinkle I always include is the unavailability of at least one key decision maker (or key technical guru). If the scenario is imagined correctly, their absence will be used to identify areas of expertise, tribal knowledge, or key decisions which are not documented or delegated and are sorely missed. In my experience, the following often comes up if the key decision maker is not available:

- Who has approval authority now for the emergency expenditures? (If the backup has a much lower limit, how does that get bumped up to cover the spend?)
- Who has authority to increase corporate credit card limits for the traveling recovery staff? (Do they even have corporate cards? If not, how do we expedite this?)
- Who else can authorize increased system access authority levels? (Who thinks through the security risks?)
- Who approves the PR statement that goes out? (Think about a canned statement with blanks to fill in with actual details so the word smiths don't take 2 days to invent the wheel.)
- What do we say about casualties and injuries?
- Can we send the hourly staff home and still pay them for the day? (On 9-11 I used HR's snow day policy to authorize this. I put on my Pirates of Penszance

Admiral's hat as the guy in charge and declared it was snowing outside!)

- Do we still pay people who can't come in because of the disaster? (What is our normal policy and if we want to make an exception, do we have the authority to do that?)
- Who can authorize unexpected overtime?
- What are our legal and contractual obligations and can we get some mercy?
- Do we notify our customers yet, and do we have to report this to a regulating authority?

If the people who make these decisions, and more, aren't available, is there a management succession plan in place which delegates the authority to make the call in their absence? Don't worry if you uncover missing elements, that's what the exercise is meant to do: expose gaps that can be remediated.

Conclusion. Without good management succession plans in place the chances are that good decisions will not be made or even thought about until it's too late. As a father, I have seen the truth in the old saying, "One child, one brain. Two children, half a brain. Three children, no brain at all." (In extreme pressure situations, some managers tend to revert to this in the middle of "groupthink".) In order to avoid confusion, conflicting agendas, and the Al Haig Syndrome, make sure everyone knows how decisions will be made in an unexpected event with key decision makers absent. Happy decision making!

CHAPTER 8

BCP FUNCTION: STAFF FROM WITHIN OR HIRE FROM OUTSIDE?

As usual, my answer is: it depends. Are you looking for a manager to build a new BCP function from the ground up, or are you looking for someone to take an existing function to the next level? If it is a new function, prior BCP experience can be very important. A good outside candidate will have a proven track record you can verify. He should have professional credentials, like a CBCP (Certified Business Continuity Planner), and solid references from their experience at building and managing a successful program. If, however, you are looking for someone to raise the existing function's game to a higher effectiveness, I would first want to know what management thinks are the shortcomings they want to improve. So let's noodle this thing through and see what we can come up with.

The benefits of hiring from within. First on the list of pros is the fact that the candidate is a known quantity with a proven track record. Check out my previous chapter on where and to whom BCP should report for guidance, but a good start is finding a good manager. Frederick Drucker, my all time favorite management consulting expert, once opined, "A manager is a manager is a manager". His point was an excellent manager can manage brain surgeons or engineers or human resources. They may be different fields, but the mechanics of good management are transferrable. A good manager will figure out the skill sets and knowledge required and create an atmosphere where his staff can shine. His job is to always keep in mind the big picture and understand the underlying requirements for a successful implementation. Second on my list of pros is someone who possesses deep company tribal knowledge. As outlined in my previous chapter, every company operates differently and has their own tribal language. An experienced manager will understand how decisions are made and by whom, how things really get done, and can make sure the BCP vision is properly communicated at all levels of the organization. All this can be hard to discern for an outsider, valuable time can be lost, and mistakes that hinder success will be made. Lastly, I would look for someone who is a quick study. BCP is not rocket science, but there are many things to learn concerning methodology, priorities, tools, and raising awareness of the importance of BCP to the company's overall risk management activities. Finding the right candidate internally can go a long way toward starting on the right foot and propelling the BCP function toward success. These points are especially true when taking over an existing, underperforming function. However, if BCP is a new effort, hiring inside has some downsides.

The cons of hiring from within. For a new function, a major hindrance would be if the candidate lacks any BCP background. At the risk of negating what I said above, being thrown into the BCP pool without prior experience can be daunting, however quick a study the candidate is. Creating a new BCP function from the ground up requires vision and a deep understanding of how to address the recovery requirements of the organization in the right priority and with the right solution set. Navigating the mine fields without significant BCP knowledge can be difficult, at best. In this situation, I would suggest buying a block of hours from an experienced consultant to help develop the Program. (Big surprise, coming from someone who makes a living doing just that, huh?) For existing functions, the cons are a little different. If the internal candidate continues to maintain significant responsibilities for other functions, as is too often the case, his efforts will be diluted and success will be harder to achieve. BCP is a big hat to wear and unless he is given the freedom to focus on the issues, the improvements of the Program's effectiveness that management is looking for may be long in coming, if they show up at all.   Also, if the candidate has spent all his time in only one silo at the company, such as the data center, he may have trouble expanding the BCP function corporate-wide, taking it from mere disaster recovery to true business continuity.

The benefits of hiring from outside.   If there are no suitable internal candidates readily available, then going to the marketplace to obtain outside talent can be the right move. Obviously, the first benefit is you are able to buy experience that someone else has paid for.   You have resumes and references to check out and thorough interviews to conduct, but if you do your vetting correctly, you can hire someone who has exactly the right background and ability to be successful, whether it is a new function or for a BCP Program that is in trouble.   It's important to set up mentoring to teach the new employee the lay of the land, but the right candidate will find his way. A second important benefit with an outside hire is the new set of eyes he brings to the situation. The outsider is exactly that, someone who should not be limited to "We've always done it that way." A fresh approach may be just what the doctor ordered. Lastly, a new hire starts with a clean slate. Having no prior history with the company, he will benefit from being given a chance to prove himself without the limitations of past performance. Most employees will give the new guy or gal the chance to be successful and some will actually be rooting for them.

The cons of hiring from the outside. All the benefits of hiring from within, as discussed above, are flipped with an outside hire. The new hire has no tribal knowledge, no proven in house connections, and no broad understanding of corporate functions and priorities. It's all new to them and they may have problems navigating toward success. Also, despite all your efforts to properly vet the candidate, some surprises may be in store. Unfortunately, you may soon figure out why he was looking for a new job in the first place, and for reasons that didn't come up in the interview process. However, if you've done your job vetting the candidate, any problems should be easy to correct and the new hire can be a great boon to the organization. Access to a good mentor should make for a smooth transition and produce the right environment for success, but it doesn't always work out the way it was intended. You pay your money and you take your chances.

Hiring the right candidate for any position is always an involved and sometimes difficult process. Finding the right person to be responsible for creating or improving the corporate BC Program is definitely worth the effort. Happy hiring.

CHAPTER 9

THE 5 BEST REASONS FOR USING A BCP CONSULTANT

Of course my favorite reason is because that's how I make enough money for my family to eat and sleep indoors. But really, there are some very good reasons to reach outside your organization for subject matter expertise and experienced help in accomplishing your BC projects. The best reasons I can think of are:

1. **A lack of internal expertise**. It may very well be that no one at your company has ever done a BCP project and there isn't a clear understanding of how to go about accomplishing the assigned mandate. A directive has come down from on high to "go forth and business contingify, whatever that is, and, by the way, you have six months." An experienced consultant can develop project focus, detail all the steps required, develop a reasonable schedule, and accomplish the tasks in the allotted time frame. A good consultant will also

major on knowledge transfer rather than building dependent step children.

2. **A lack of internal resources**.   It's especially true in smaller organizations, but most companies operate on a rather lean staff budget and they don't have a pool of technical and business people sitting around with large open areas in their job description just waiting to take on a project of this magnitude.   The leader of the project usually has an already crowded plate and nothing gets removed to make time for this new responsibility.   A good consultant is a dedicated resource who can focus entirely on the project and should bring not just direction but strong shoulders to carry the bulk of the weight.   I tell prospective clients, "I hire people to do things like wallpaper the kitchen because I have too many Howard things to do. Assign me part of your to do list so you can focus on the stuff that only you can do. Give me this project and I'll get it done, and make you look smart for hiring me."

3. **People tend to cooperate with outside consultants**. The staff usually realizes the company is paying for this consultant and so they should probably cooperate so whoever brought them in doesn't get a report that they have become a roadblock. Like many families, they treat outsiders with a little more deference than they would one of their own. This is not always the case, but a good consultant recognizes the obstacles and uses his powers of persuasion to get on calendars, run meetings efficiently, gather information as painlessly as possible, and honor everyone's time pressures.

4. **A good consultant brings a deep well of experience**. This BCP project is not their first rodeo, or least it shouldn't be or you've got the wrong consultant. They may have even done similar projects at similar companies in the same industry. They should be able to provide insight on how your peers are doing BCP and be able to cross pollinate solutions and recovery methods from other industries as well. The consultant should be able to enrich the solution set with lessons learned on successful efforts

performed elsewhere. They should have a clear understanding of the technology required to support the client's recovery needs and priorities, a handle on realistic expectations for the time required for recovery, an ability to outline effective recovery strategies, and the ability to build the business case for BC/DR expenditures. He should also be able to identify a roadmap for the way forward to improved recovery capabilities (not just upsell opportunities for his firm). And, perhaps it goes without saying, he should have a good handle on project management metrics including adequate status reporting on the project's progress and unresolved issues.

5. **Company budgets often have restrictions on hiring new staff**. Even though the BCP project has high level support and has been deemed an important requirement for this year, the bean counters have convinced management that the people costs are the easiest and most important to control. The edict comes down, "No more hires this year", and the door for adding skilled staff slams shut. You'd like to go out and find an experienced BC

person to bring onboard, but that is not possible.   However, consultant dollars often come from a different budget and since the project has a defined cost and duration, money becomes available to bring in an outsider to handle a short term project. When the project is over, he goes away and you are not saddled with the cost of an ongoing head count.

In a future blog on my website I will discuss how to find and use a good consultant, but for now let me just encourage you to make use of the wealth of experience a good consultant has learned while someone else was paying for acquiring that knowledge. I realize mine is not an entirely objective opinion (my professional motto is, after all, *"Consulteo ergo sum"* **I consult therefore I am**), but I believe the right consultant can be a tremendous resource for the success of your BC project. As always, I welcome your comments and please feel free to contact me. Good projects to you.

CHAPTER 10

WHO WRITES THE BC AND DR PLANS?

Okay, so you're the internal Business Continuity subject matter expert (SME) for your company. That means you're supposed to write all the plans: disaster recovery plans for the data center, network recovery plans, voice and data plans, etc., plus all the business continuity plans for each of the business functions, right?   Wrong, in my humble opinion.   While I agree you are probably the most qualified, if you write all these plans by yourself they become, ipso facto, **your** plans. You wrote them, you own them.   You'll get very little buy in by those who have to execute them at time of disaster.   So I encourage BC planners to think more as facilitators and project managers that draw heavily on the involvement of others to accomplish a group goal rather than operate as a sole contributor. As the BCP SME, you are in an excellent position to design the format of the plans and then facilitate the cooperation of the other area SME's to provide the content from both the technical and business sides of the house. Let me explain what I mean.

Disaster Recovery Plans. The technical side of the house should provide documentation, procedures, priorities, and the recovery timeline. They have a vested interest in the recovery process and often have to respond to various minor outages on a short time schedule, so their awareness of the need of written recovery plans is usually high because of past experience. Even if you have deep technical knowledge, involve others to provide the content of the plans. If you design a good format, they can easily fill in the blanks. And remember, a lot of the procedures only reside in their collective grey matter and have never been written down. Put on your consultant hat and guide them through the process of creating a plan that can be accomplished with or without them being available. That way they'll own their section of the recovery and will tend to keep things up to date without your continued haranguing.

Business Continuity Plans. Business function staff are usually not predisposed to thinking about unexpected outages. You've seen their deer in the headlights look when there's no dial tone, or the systems freeze up, or they have to leave the building. They need your help in designing and implementing their outage and recovery responses, but resist the temptation to do it all for them. I encourage BC SME's to use the BIA process to get them to begin thinking about how they can continue mission critical functions without the support they've come to depend upon. (I refer to this as "evangelizing among the heathen" as you open their eyes to the fact they are expected to function as best they can during an outage to continue the mission.) As the SME's for their area they are intimately familiar with the processes that must be accomplished, the priorities that will change during an outage, workflow changes, critical staff, etc. I suggest you hold a planning workshop for them and explain the format and content they will have to supply. (If you leave it up to them, you'll get anything from a three ring binder to notes on a cocktail napkin.) But with your guidance, they will be able to write a plan that is truly theirs and will address all their requirements during the outage. I also encourage you to hold a tabletop exercise so they can educate their staff on what will be expected of them, work through any missing elements, and will they'll feel the importance of what they are doing. This will happen much more so than if you wrote the plan and dropped it off like the Sunday newspaper delivery.

Conclusion. For some BCP SME's it is a new thought to see themselves as facilitators rather than chief scribes. But I firmly believe that a feeling of ownership of the plans is a very important element of successful implementation during recovery efforts. With you acting as a consultant, the end product is more thorough, precise, complete, and stands a good chance of surviving the initial shock of an unexpected outage, especially if those called upon to execute the plan were the chief authors.   Happy planning!

CHAPTER 11

SELLING MANAGEMENT TRAINEES ON JOINING THE BCP TEAM.

Many modern corporations have instituted a management training program full of bright young college graduates that circulate through various departments to gain experience and operational knowledge in preparation for their careers. They usually have some choice in determining which departments they intern with. The question is: how do you attract them to your Business Continuity Program (BCP) as one of their assignments? Since you asked, here is how I have done it several times in my own career.

Sell the BCP Function. It's vital that you sell them on the importance of what you do. They will probably never have been exposed to the business continuity discipline, but they all live technology-dependent lives. They've all experienced broken cell phones, laptops on the fritz, and application problems. What the BCP deals with is all that, and more, writ large. It will be easy for you to explain that the BCP is the guardian of the availability of essential corporate resources and you're the ones who figure out what do to in the face of unexpected outages.   Having experienced technology failings in their own lives, they will quickly grasp the importance of preserving access to the tools and data the company depends upon to continue mission critical functions.

Sell the BCP View. The Program touches all aspects of operations, administration, and facilities in ways few other departments do. Because of the broad corporate-wide scope they will have an in depth view into all the corporation's essential activities and assets. By being involved in the Business Impact Analysis (BIA) for a business function they will learn all about the department's mission critical activities and will understand how it relates to information systems and other departments.   By being involved in the development of business continuity and disaster recovery planning they will have a ringside seat in watching the areas struggle with how they will continue those functions in the face of unexpected outages. Because the BCP addresses issues in all areas, they will have a wonderful opportunity to acquire firsthand knowledge of so much more than they would by sitting in a cubicle in some other department. (The BCP is, in fact, a step ladder in the cubicle farm.) They can also use the assignment to scope out where they want to land next. By then, they will have had a chance to meet the department management and gained the ability to take a lot of the guesswork out of whether they would like to intern there or not.

Sell the Management Exposure. Because of the important issues BCP deals with, they will have the opportunity to attend meetings with senior management across the organization. I often prepped my trainees for speaking and writing roles that gave them the kind of exposure interning in Accounting never would have done. I told them that shining in BCP could do wonders for their future careers. When their interning days are over, they will have had direct contact with the corporate decision makers and can approach them with a pitch to join their team, rather than cold calling.

Conclusion. BCP managers rarely tap the wealth of talent that resides in the management training pool, to their loss, I believe. By attracting great talent, treating them well, and giving them the view and exposure that will help them in their future careers, you will have a great resource to use for a while. You will also be making allies for the future who understand the importance of what you do. Who knows, the future CFO or HR Director may turn out to be one of your alumni down the road.

Happy selling!

CHAPTER 12

5 IMPORTANT BC QUESTIONS TO ASK FOR MERGERS & ACQUISITIONS

It seems every day there is a new announcement about one company buying another one. Sometimes the target company is a competitor, other times it will be a company that will enable the buyer to complement or expand their portfolio of services or products. (For example, Verizon bought CyberTrust to acquire our extensive portfolio of professional services.) An early stage of the M&A courtship is the Due Diligence phase, where the buyer sizes up the target, checks the books, reviews production, and details assets. If everything looks good and the price is right, they walk the aisle together.

What does BC have to do with M&A? I'm glad you asked. Here are what I believe are 5 important BC-related questions that should a part of every M&A effort and should be asked of the target company:

1. **Do they have an active contract with a BC/DR vendor, and is it assumable**? If the target company has

a valid contract with a vendor it may represent an ongoing legal agreement and financial obligation that may not end with the purchase, or maybe can't be assumed by the buyer if it so desires. Depending on the integration plans the buyer intends to implement, the arrangement may still be necessary for a length of time (and may need to be extended) or it could be unnecessary or redundant. Often times this is overlooked during the Due Diligence Phase and could turn out to be an unpleasant surprise later, effecting the actual cost of integration. (Always remember, management doesn't like M&A surprises!)

2. **Do they have trained BC/DR staff?** It has been my experience that those companies that do poor due diligence often don't recognize the value of staff they are acquiring. By not addressing personnel issues right up front they find the cream of the crop walking out the door, taking their valuable skills and tribal knowledge with them, and are left with the less nimble folks who have fewer options, and maybe less skill and knowledge. Finding a trained staff who

can implement a successful BC/DR program can be a valuable asset when evaluating the talent about to join the mothership.

3. **Are there any assets that can be used to augment the buyer's recovery capabilities?** Many M&A methodologies overlook technology and physical assets that would be a wonderful addition to the resources available to improve recoverability for the buyer. Instead of sending everything to a landfill in New Jersey or selling it for pennies on the dollar, the M&A team should be encouraged to keep an eye out for what seems to be redundant resources that could be used to upgrade the buyer's current state of recovery and integrate new capabilities that will be needed for the newly acquired operations. Equipment I always look for includes telephone switches, servers, disc farms, tape management systems, routers, generators, UPS, and HVAC equipment. I also want to take a look at their facilities in case I find a great place to create a new cold/warm site, or find useful alternate telecommunications and power pathways, or provide an offsite

business area recovery capability. Like sorting through a flea market or attic, you may find the technology equivalent of a Mickey Mantle rookie year baseball card.

4. **Have they done a recent Business Impact Analysis?** A good BIA will tell the buyer what the most critical business processes are at the target and will help set expectations for priorities for the integration phase and ongoing recovery requirements and capabilities. I have on a number of occasions also used the ISO standards to review security and recovery concerns at acquisition targets to get a better feel for what problems might come along before the buyer's name goes on the wall.

5. **How will the acquisition change recovery requirements at the buyer?** If the acquisition goes through, it will inevitably change the scope and perhaps the way in which the buyer plans for disaster recovery and business continuity. The new addition to the company fold will bring with it new equipment, connectivity needs, business areas, and perhaps facilities. For

example, the target may bring with them 100 new servers. Some of those servers may support critical operations that require immediate failover where none currently exists in the buyer's backup location. Getting out in front of these costs will go a long way to determine just how great a deal this was. Including these expenditures during the Due Diligence Phase can help to effect a number of decisions regarding price, data center expansion, and additional recovery costs.

Therefore, I always encourage the BC/DR manager to sit down with the M&A team to present these questions for inclusion in their due diligence methodology. Getting them to keep an eye out for this information you need, along with your potential shopping list, will increase the BC Program's visibility and will perform a valuable contribution to a successful merger. Involvement in the M&A process will prevent a merger diluting the current state recovery capability and can serve to enhance and expand it. At the very least, BC/DR will get to look over the loot before it disappears out the door. Please feel free to make comments and offer your own suggestions and war stories.   And, as always, feel free to contact me directly.   Happy merging and acquiring.

CHAPTER 13

12 KEYS TO A SUCCESSFUL TABLETOP EXERCISE

I am a firm believer in the usefulness of tabletop exercises in testing all facets of disaster recovery and business continuity plans. I tell my customers, "Every watch is waterproof until you dunk it." The worst case scenario for a customer is to have to exercise their recovery plans for real during an actual outage without first having tested their assumptions, documentation, and procedures in the safe environment of a conference room as a drill. The lessons to be learned and the training of staff obtained during a walkthrough of the plans is absolutely critical to ensure the plans can survive, as the military calls it, the heat of battle.

In conducting a successful test the planners should keep the following 12 elements in mind:

1. **Plan the scope of the test carefully**. The tabletop test should last no more than 4 hours, so you will not have time to test every possible pathway of the plan, but you should major on the important aspects of recovery. The old

chestnut, "Don't boil the ocean" seems appropriate. If you're testing the data center disaster recovery plan, you might want to simply address the first and second tier of applications and the resources they require. If it's a business continuity plan, you might want to limit the test to just a few business areas and their most critical functions. If the test becomes too involved, there is a tendency to get bogged down and the time will run out before you've covered everything you wanted to hit.

2. **Determine what a successful test looks like**. Make a complete list of all the aspects of the plan you want to test and what constitutes a successful completion of those tasks. For example, if you want the technical staff to walk through bringing the applications up in the recovery environment, have them go through their written documentation, step by step, and look for any missing elements that are not included in the documentation. Pay attention to timing, priorities, and dependencies. If it's a business area continuity plan, have them work through the action steps they must take before, during, and after the systems are restored. You'll want to hear about how they ascertain the

application and data has been restored correctly and how they would handle unexpected delays. (In effect, they are simulating turnover testing.) In tabletop exercises, always bear in mind that finding missing elements is a good thing. It makes the plan that much better when the remediation efforts are done.

3. **Educate the participants on what to expect.** People make excuses to miss meetings when they don't know what will happen there, and tabletops are no exception. Send out a memo detailing what will happen (they'll be walking through their plans to respond to a scenario that will be revealed at the start of the test), the purpose of the tabletop (to improve recoverability by ensuring the documentation and procedures are complete and accurate), the scope of the test, the elements of a successful test in this case, and who will be participating. Pre-warned is pre-armed. If they know what to expect, the likelihood of them being prepared to fully participate is increased dramatically.

4. **Create a meaningful outage scenario that could really happen.** Don't use, "So, Mars attacks" or you'll lose them right from the beginning and you'll never

get them back. What you want is a realistic scenario that could reasonably happen that will test the various legs of the plan. For example, you could use a fire in one of the facilities, a sudden loss of power or telecom from an errant backhoe (it's happened to me twice before), a regional weather-related disaster (hurricanes, snowstorms, floods, etc.), an electrical loss in a building due to an accident that causes a hard data center crash (again, another real experience of mine involving a workman, a step ladder, and the emergency power off switch), or an extensive Denial of Service attack. You want something that would cause a disaster declaration that calls for immediate response so you can begin walking through the recovery steps. You can plan to insert new mitigating circumstances as the day goes on, like the fire damage being worse than initially expected, but don't over complicate it to the point where you frustrate the responders.

5. **Keep the scenario secret**. Real disasters, except maybe hurricanes, don't come with warnings and your goal is to measure how effectively the participants are able to respond to an unexpected outage. This may be an

open-book test (the plans), but the outage scenario they will need to operate under should remain unknown until the test begins, just like in real life. Several years ago I worked with a large retail chain to conduct their annual hurricane prep tabletop. They knew the scenario would be a hurricane strike somewhere in their footprint, but they had no idea what stores might be effected, what highways might be flooded, which airports were closed, what warehouse might be damaged, etc. Since I was also a stock holder, not just a consultant, I made sure the test scenario had a few surprises in store. I was protecting my investment.

6. **Watch out for key staff dependencies.** Every company has one or two key staffers who are the holders of tribal knowledge nobody else has. Or they hold the decision making authority tightly, and if they're not available (something you might include in your scenario), recovery grinds to a halt or is significantly slowed. During a tabletop for a rural electrical authority in Georgia I noticed the staff would frequently turn to Bob and ask, "Where do we keep that stuff, or who do we call about that." I went to the blackboard and wrote

WWBD. Naturally, they asked, "What's that?" I told them, "You know that WWJD stands for What Would Jesus Do. Well, you have a Bob problem because there are too many questions you ask What Would Bob Do. If Bob was on vacation, or unavailable, you'd be up the river without a paddle." I suggested they interview Bob extensively and find out what information resided only in his grey cells and not on paper, and write it down in the plans. At a conference I was speaking at several months later, one of them came up to me and said, "Bob retired last month and we're really glad you had us interview him because we found out lots of stuff only he knew because he was around for so many years".

7. **Keep the exercise on track**. Nature, and people, abhor a vacuum, so if you don't stick closely to the agenda. someone will always take over and point the discussion where he wants it to go. At the risk of appearing rude, you'll have to cut some discussions short or redirect attention back to the scenario and the tasks at hand. Make a note if something needs further examination, but don't let

the test grind to a halt to solve a single problem.

8. **Walkthrough the plans as written.** Call on individuals to read through their task lists as currently written and make note of missing elements. Remember, you're attempting to validate the plans that are before you and find out if they are complete and accurate. So if someone says, "We'd follow the restart procedures for loading the data base for such and such", you want to ask, "Are those procedures written down, and if they're not directly in your documentation, is there a link to where we would get them and would they be available if the systems were down." All the tasks should include an expected timeframe in which they are intended to be accomplished so you can watch for bottlenecks in the recovery process should those tasks be delayed.

9. **Record any open issues or missing documentation.** You'll need scribe support to record all the activities and especially to capture missing elements or problems that need to be solved later. I usually start a list on the whiteboard to capture these issues and assign

responsibility and a due date for resolution. A good tabletop will discover these and you don't want to lose them or fail to assign someone to get the answers or write the missing documentation.

10.   **End on time.** Always remember that these people have a lot of other things they could (should) be doing, but they've given you the time to attend and participate at a cost to themselves and their regular job.   Respect for their commitment means wrapping things up according to the agenda, so keep an eye on the clock and include a drop dead time for yourself to begin bringing closure to the test activities. Leave time for a brief summation, a review of the open issues, and a hearty thanks for their time and participation. Do it right, and they won't call in sick the next time you schedule a test.

11.   **Write an after action report and circulate it to the participants and management.**   Include   the preparations, the announcement memo (maybe in the appendix), the scenario, a description of the test activities, lessons learned, and the open issues and assignments. Remember you've just tied

up 10-30 staff members for a half day and you need to give an account of what was accomplished. You want to use the after action report to convince management that the exercise was worth the effort. You want to demonstrate that real progress was made at ensuring the organization is continuing to improve on its ability to respond to unexpected outages in the timeframes required by critical business processes.

12.   **Update the plan and track the assignments**. Make sure all the missing elements and open issues are addressed and the plans have been updated to include the lessons learned during the tabletop. At some time in the future issue a follow up report that details the progress made and makes management aware of any remaining open issues or missed due dates.

Tabletop exercises are an important BC/DR tool that should not be overlooked. The experience serves to improve plans, generate new ideas, and train the staff that will be called upon to exercise the recovery tasks in a real outage. You can get a lot done in a conference room that will make the real world easier to bear. Happy testing!

CHAPTER 14

BC/DR AND THE CORPORATE SDLC

Last year I had the opportunity to meet a senior member of a former client's executive management team while we both spoke at a conference in Miami. I began by asking him if they still did a Peace Business Continuity BIA before any new system was put in place. He smiled at me and said, "So you're the guy who worked with so and so back in 2000."

One of my priorities then and now was to insert BC/DR considerations into the System Development Life Cycle (SDLC) so they would be addressed up front. There are some very important reasons for doing this.

Every major change should be preceded by a focused BIA. A properly conducted BIA for the change will identify what new pressures will be brought to bear on the current state recovery strategy. New applications, business functions, and infrastructure changes can have a discrete and, perhaps, debilitating impact on disaster recovery strategies and business continuity planning. The BIA should be used to measure outage impacts for the new change and be used to measure the overall impact on recovery requirements. If the SDLC includes a BIA hook, it'll happen.

Each BIA Impact Category should have a list of recovery requirements. For example, at the client mentioned above, I used the categories we developed in our Y2K work to separate the most critical (AAA) from the more deferrable (D). I then used the categories to delineate what recovery requirements each new application needed to include in their planning. For the AAA through B ratings, the developers were required to include local failover (multi-processor environment), remote failover at the recovery instance, written recovery plans for the application and business units supported, and annual failover recovery testing. Putting those requirements early in the SDLC made for far better upfront planning and trying to retrofit them later would have been impossible. It eliminates the 'but nobody told us" excuse.

BC/DR considerations must be included in the budget. The final price has to include provisions for recovery from the very beginning because there will be no money available later. For example, a new AAA application will be required to run in a multi-processor environment for local failover, not a single-threaded server, and another one is needed in the recovery environment. Now we're talking about two specialized servers, not one and some possible impact on the network response time. The project budget should include this additional capability. Pricing things right in the beginning will mean an accurate assessment of the true costs.

A Gap Analysis should be performed to determine the overall impact of the change. The current state recovery capabilities should be examined to determine if the change will open any gaps in the company's ability to recover critical business functions in the timeframe required. The change can impact the data center, data and voice networks, and business area recovery, or all of the above. Any gaps discovered can affect budgets and project delivery timeframes and priorities.

Here is what you're trying to accomplish: At some opportune point between the time some executive says, "That's a great idea" and the time they reach for their wallet, you want BC/DR considerations to be addressed so the real price is known and the implementation plan is written accurately. If there are BC/DR hooks in the SDLC, all the recovery issues are addressed in a timely fashion and the fixes won't need to be bolted on later, if at all. Happy SDLC'ing.

CHAPTER 15

5 WAYS CONSULTING RESEMBLES CURLING

Okay, so for those who didn't grow up with 3 channel black and white TV in the fifties, Curling is a Canadian sport involving ice, brooms, and large tubs. (For those from NYC, think of ice Bocce.) When I was a kid a thousand years ago, Curling used to come on one of the snowy channels we got and the season started after football season in the old days, before the playoffs extended to Valentine's Day. In fact, Curling is now an Olympic sport, if you can believe it, and can be interesting to watch if you understand the rules. It occurred to me several years ago that Curling and consulting are the same sport. Keep reading. I promise to make sense of my analogy.

Curling begins behind a start line where a player moves forward and lowers the moving tub onto the ice with the goal of hitting a target 100 feet away. If the tub moves too fast, or if it strikes the target too hard, it will careen outside the scoring circle and the fans will shout obscene comments on the players' ability and family heritage. The pace and direction of the tub down the ice is influenced by two players with brooms who will sweep the ice ahead of it in order to change direction and speed to enable it to hit the target and remain in scoring position, unless it is pushed aside by the opposing team. Got it? Now let's compare the game to consulting.

1. Every BCP consulting engagement has a target, whether it is a Business Impact Analysis, or a Business Continuity Plan, or a Disaster Recovery Test. It is conducted often on a rather slippery field with outside influences, some beyond your control, which will attempt to effect the outcome. Some of the players will have separate agendas entirely and some of your players will not be very adept at keeping things on target. The difference between curling and consulting is, unfortunately, that the target can move if it isn't written in stone in the Statement of Work (SOW). Mission creep outside the scoring zone is a real possibility if you're not careful.

2. BCP Consulting engagements are a team sport. Any consultant who thinks he can

accomplish the target without help will have no supporting players to keep the goal firmly in mind and the project on track. Cultivate cooperation toward your shared goal. Remember you are there to help your team navigate the mine fields and produce a mutually beneficial result. You are there to serve, not rule.

3. <u>As in curling, consultants are not allowed to smack the tub with the broom to keep it on track</u>. This is sometimes very tempting, but don't do it. It's against the rules. Treat every opinion with respect, no matter how idiotic, and work hard at gaining consensus. Resist pontificating on BCP dogma and project management methodology and you'll stand a better chance of hitting the target. Always remember, you can drywall with a sledgehammer but the cleanup is messy. You can make your point without leaving a gaping divot.

4. <u>Use influence by getting out in front of the project</u>. That's what the brooms are for, influencing the project by smoothing the way toward the goal. You can use influence by subtly arranging the way for things to go at the speed and direction

which will accomplish your goals. Recognize the staff power structure and the important players and enlist their help in keeping the project on target. Inexperienced consultants need to learn how to convince already busy people to do one more damned thing, for them. Consultants who don't do "subtle" are rarely successful and don't get return engagements.

5. <u>The game is over when the official (client) says so</u>. Sure, I have had clients that were like Lt. Colombo ("Ah, one more thing...") and they've tried to drag the project out before final approval (and payment). But always remember your goal is to deliver an end product that's sits squarely in scoring position. The client should be confident that he got what he paid for and that his goals, not just yours, were reached. For me, the most efficient way to accomplish this is through consistent feedback throughout the project and vetting both the data and the conclusions. Don't drop your final report off like a drive by newspaper delivery. Use drafts and rewrites until you both know your data collection is complete and accurate and that any

conclusions and recommendations make sense and are on target. No surprises. I learned this while doing bank risk reviews for Lloyds of London in Latin America. At the end of the week, I would have all my findings and recommendations written down and would meet with the board of directors to lay it all out for them. Any changes that needed to be made were made with them so there would be no surprises when London took my report and made the recommendations requirements for renewed insurance coverage. If you take the same approach, you will have much happier clients and they will consider you for future engagements.

Hopefully, this advice makes sense and will help you to leave the clients happy and cheering as you hit the target and scored a successful project conclusion. And remember, the same analogy works for internal projects if you are an employee. Use persuasion and don't just rely on policy to gain cooperation. Leave me any comments you might have on my website, including any correction of my insight into a fine Canadian sport. Happy consulting!

CHAPTER 16

THE JOYS AND TRIALS OF THE CONSULTING LIFE

Whenever anyone asks my wife what I do for a living, she replies "He's a pooper scooper. He solves problems no one else knows how to solve." I try to get her to say my job is to make mountains into speed bumps, but I can't really argue with her description. As a consultant, I am usually hired to bring my subject matter expertise to bear on an internal problem that, for some reason, no one at my client has the knowledge, experience, or time to solve. Sometimes it's to offer advice and at other times it's to do the heavy lifting. After decades of consulting, I have found I've gotten better and better at it and come to really enjoy the process. First, let me tell you why I think it is an important field and why I think it's fun.

Exposure to new industries. Over the years I've been exposed to a multitude of industries I never would have otherwise seen up close. I've consulted with clients who manufacture bricks, truck axles, electronics, clothing, pet supplies, and a myriad of other items. I've worked with clients who manage retail store chains, rental car outlets, and large distribution networks. I've consulted with technology companies, voice and data carriers, banks, credit card companies, credit unions, software vendors, hospitals, labor management firms, and government branches. Every industry has different processes, products, and priorities, but the tools I use, especially the Business Impact Analysis (BIA), have opened my eyes to the inner workings that either make the client successful or hinders their progress. I never tire of the learning process and have been blessed to see much, much more than I would have sitting in a cubicle for 30 years.

Exposure to new people. I love meeting and working with new people. I regard new contacts as presents I get to unwrap. Some wonderful friendships have evolved over the years and among my clients and coworkers have been some of the brightest people I have ever met. Exposure to them has made me all the richer in knowledge and friendship because of it.

Exposure to new knowledge and methods. In addition to learning about their industries, I've been exposed to better ways to do a number of the things I was supposed to be the expert at. There are many ways to crack a nut and I've often found that great ideas and methods are available if I'll only pay close attention to what is being said and done already. I warn my clients that I'm a shameless stealer of good ideas and am always on the prowl for better ways of doing what I do for a living.

Exposure to new problems and solutions. More than once I've stood there scratching my head over a roadblock I'd never encountered before. Being challenged with a new problem always gets my juices flowing and I enjoy the satisfaction of standing back after solving it and seeing a job well done.

Opportunities to teach. I am a consultant that is committed to knowledge transfer. I have no interest in building dependent step children, so I work hard at equipping my clients to carry on successfully after I leave. I often will explain the "why's" and not just the "what's" about the project so the results can have lasting impact and be improved over time.

Travel to new places. Have you seen that Facebook app that has you click off all the states you've visited? I was really surprised at all the places my consulting career has taken me. I only missed the Dakotas, but there's still time. Maybe I have some Gypsy blood, but I have definitely enjoyed crisscrossing the country and going overseas as a paid tourist.

Okay, now it's time to look at the downsides of consulting. My wife likes to say, "There are bedpans in every job, and some days are bedpan days". So, in fairness, let's look at some of those.

The hardships of travel. Air travel has become increasingly more difficult in the years since 9/11. The lines are longer, security is much more onerous, carryon bags are smaller, and most flights are full, the seating is cramped and not laptop friendly (and why do corporate travel departments always stick you in a middle seat or in the one next to the bathroom at the very back of the plane?). When you arrive, you race to pick up the rental car and set about finding your hotel in a new city you don't know. Depending on your per diem, you may find yourself staying at a Motel 4 and might have trouble finding restaurants that serve edible meals within your budget. When people tell me I'm so lucky to travel for a living, I tell them, "If you only knew...."

Being away from home. When my son was young, my wife used to say all the exciting things happened when I was away and not able to help (like the time he got bit by a chipmunk). Besides missing my family, I also missed out on being able to do some of the chores around the house at night so the honey-do list built up all week and Saturday became a work like a slave day. When you travel you also miss out on after school events and time with friends, and maybe date night with your wife. The good thing about properly managing the travel, however, was that I was often able to be on site with a client for a week, get my arms around as much stuff as I could, and then work from home for a week or two before going back out the door.

Leaving your best work behind. I've had a number of projects that I was really satisfied with and would have loved to see how it all got worked out in the days ahead. It would have been very rewarding to be around to see the fruits of my labor get fully implemented, but I had to move on to the next client. I was able to leave them with a roadmap for going forward, but I wasn't going to be there to see it taken to the next level. And as a consultant you always wonder if they're going to take that report with all the great recommendations and stick it on the shelf as though you were never there.

So, as you can see, there are great joys and substantial downsides to being a consultant. For me, the joys have always outweighed the negatives and I'm still having fun. Leave me some comments and feel free to contact me directly on my website at www.peacebusinesscontinuity.com. Happy consulting, and be safe out there.

EPILOGUE

First, I want to thank you for reading this book. I hope it has been helpful as well as entertaining. There are many other books out there on the subject and many of them are designed to be authoritative, step by step approaches, but that is probably not my strength. As a consultant, I wanted to share personal insights, opinions, and war stories about my long career in BC/DR. My goal was to make it like a couple of people talking over dinner, exploring the ups and downs, the roadblocks, and the joys of working in this field. Hopefully, I've accomplished that.

To continue our conversation, please access my website at www.peacebusinesscontinuity.com to read further blog insights and feel free to leave comments, email me, or give me a call. (I'm thinking about adding a service called "Rent a Grey Head" where clients can buy a block of time by the hour, but that is not intended to prevent fellow professionals from getting me on the phone for a good long chat.) If I can help in anyway, please don't hesitate to contact me. I hope you enjoy the BC field as much as I have. Peace!